IF YOU FOUND THIS BOOK, PLEASE RETURN IT TO:

NAME: _____

PHONE: _____

EMAIL: _____

ADDRESS: _____

_____

THANK YOU FOR YOUR PURCHASE

EMAIL US AT:

customers@gracefulbydesign.com

TO SHARE YOUR EXPERIENCE, WISHES FOR IMPROVEMENTS, OR SIMPLY HOW YOU ARE ENJOYING THIS PRODUCT OR ANY OF OUR GRACEFUL BY DESIGN PRODUCTS.

FOLLOW US ON INSTAGRAM

@gracefulbydesignllc

FOR NEW PRODUCT RELEASES, AS WELL AS SALES INFORMATION. WANT TO HELP OUR SMALL BUSINESS GROW? TAG US IN A COMMENT OR PICTURE OF HOW YOU ARE USING OUR PRODUCTS.

VISIT **www.gracefulbydesign.com**

FOR MORE INFORMATION OR TO SIGN UP FOR OUR GRACEFUL BY DESIGN NEWSLETTER.

A NOTE TO THE HOMESCHOOLING PARENT

In the last five years of homeschooling my children, I have gone through more planners than years I have taught. Unfortunately, I couldn't find one with everything I needed and ended up with a mess of added papers trying to keep track of all we need as a homeschool educator. My goal with creating this planner was to include everything you could possibly need to help organize the chaos that can occur in teaching young minds. Every child and every homeschool is different, so feel free to complete only some parts of this planner that apply to your homeschool. I would love to hear what you find most valuable and what you do not as we continue to grow as a small business. My hope for your family homeschool is that this helps to provoke thought and create some comfort in a routine, but also to help build time efficiencies throughout your very busy days. As you veteran homeschool educators know, some days will go as planned, and some will not. Some of our family's most beautiful and memorable schooling days were done outside our regular schedule. This planner is a guide to help you, as the teacher, and your students, have a written view of your plans and goals for this year. Remember to be flexible; this planner aims to reduce stress, not add it. May you have a blessed year ahead. I will leave you with a reminder I still need daily; you are enough!

Sincerely, Jenna

Graceful
BY DESIGN

Copyright © 2023, Graceful by Design. All rights reserved. No part of this publication may be reproduced, stored, distributed, or transmitted in any form or by any means without prior written permission of the publisher, except in the case of brief quotations embodied in critical reviews and certain other non-commercial uses permitted by copyright law. All rights reserved worldwide.

TABLE OF CONTENTS

Goal Setting for the year — pg. 6

Field Trip Planner — pg. 14

Yearly and Quarterly Overview of the Year (6) — pg. 16

Weekly Student Schedules (6) — pg. 22

Teacher's Master Schedule — pg. 28

12 Months of Lesson Planning: — pg. 30

- Monthly Overview
- Monthly Calendar and Family Hydration Tracker
- Weekly Lesson Plans

References & Records: — pg. 200

- State/Local Requirements & Contact information
- Educational websites
- Grade keepers (6)
- Attendance Tracker (6)
- Book Log (6)
- Family Chore Chart
- Curriculum & Supplies Tracker
- Motivational Quotes and Verses
- Notes Pages

OUR HOMESCHOOL GOALS

WORDS OR VERSE TO LIVE BY THIS YEAR...

THINGS TO LEARN	THINGS TO TRY
PLACES TO GO	PEOPLE TO MEET
HABITS TO BREAK	HABITS TO CREATE

GOALS FOR THE YEAR

NAME: _____ AGE: _____

SPIRITUAL

PERSONAL

ACADEMIC

RELATIONAL

GOALS FOR THE YEAR

NAME: .... AGE: ....

SPIRITUAL

PERSONAL

ACADEMIC

RELATIONAL

GOALS FOR THE YEAR

NAME: _____ AGE: _____

SPIRITUAL

PERSONAL

ACADEMIC

RELATIONAL

GOALS FOR THE YEAR

NAME: AGE:

SPIRITUAL

PERSONAL

ACADEMIC

RELATIONAL

GOALS FOR THE YEAR

NAME: _____ AGE: _____

SPIRITUAL

PERSONAL

ACADEMIC

RELATIONAL

GOALS FOR THE YEAR

NAME: .... AGE: ....

SPIRITUAL

PERSONAL

ACADEMIC

RELATIONAL

HOMESCHOOLING ALLOWS YOU THE FREEDOM TO STEP OFF THE HIGHWAY OF LEARNING AND TAKE A MORE SCENIC ROUTE ALONG A DIRT ROAD

TAMARA CHILVER

FIELD TRIPS

JANUARY
WHEN
WHERE
CONTACT

FEBRUARY
WHEN
WHERE
CONTACT

MARCH
WHEN
WHERE
CONTACT

JULY
WHEN
WHERE
CONTACT

AUGUST
WHEN
WHERE
CONTACT

SEPTEMBER
WHEN
WHERE
CONTACT

FIELD TRIPS

APRIL
WHEN
WHERE
CONTACT

MAY
WHEN
WHERE
CONTACT

JUNE
WHEN
WHERE
CONTACT

OCTOBER
WHEN
WHERE
CONTACT

NOVEMBER
WHEN
WHERE
CONTACT

DECEMBER
WHEN
WHERE
CONTACT

YEARLY OVERVIEW

STUDENT: _____

1ST QUARTER	2ND QUARTER	3RD QUARTER	4TH QUARTER
WEEK 1	WEEK 10	WEEK 19	WEEK 28
WEEK 2	WEEK 11	WEEK 20	WEEK 29
WEEK 3	WEEK 12	WEEK 21	WEEK 30
WEEK 4	WEEK 13	WEEK 22	WEEK 31
WEEK 5	WEEK 14	WEEK 23	WEEK 32
WEEK 6	WEEK 15	WEEK 24	WEEK 33
WEEK 7	WEEK 16	WEEK 25	WEEK 34
WEEK 8	WEEK 17	WEEK 26	WEEK 35
WEEK 9	WEEK 18	WEEK 27	WEEK 36

YEARLY OVERVIEW

STUDENT: _____

1ST QUARTER	2ND QUARTER	3RD QUARTER	4TH QUARTER
WEEK 1	WEEK 10	WEEK 19	WEEK 28
WEEK 2	WEEK 11	WEEK 20	WEEK 29
WEEK 3	WEEK 12	WEEK 21	WEEK 30
WEEK 4	WEEK 13	WEEK 22	WEEK 31
WEEK 5	WEEK 14	WEEK 23	WEEK 32
WEEK 6	WEEK 15	WEEK 24	WEEK 33
WEEK 7	WEEK 16	WEEK 25	WEEK 34
WEEK 8	WEEK 17	WEEK 26	WEEK 35
WEEK 9	WEEK 18	WEEK 27	WEEK 36

YEARLY OVERVIEW

STUDENT: _____

1ST QUARTER	2ND QUARTER	3RD QUARTER	4TH QUARTER
WEEK 1	WEEK 10	WEEK 19	WEEK 28
WEEK 2	WEEK 11	WEEK 20	WEEK 29
WEEK 3	WEEK 12	WEEK 21	WEEK 30
WEEK 4	WEEK 13	WEEK 22	WEEK 31
WEEK 5	WEEK 14	WEEK 23	WEEK 32
WEEK 6	WEEK 15	WEEK 24	WEEK 33
WEEK 7	WEEK 16	WEEK 25	WEEK 34
WEEK 8	WEEK 17	WEEK 26	WEEK 35
WEEK 9	WEEK 18	WEEK 27	WEEK 36

YEARLY OVERVIEW

STUDENT: _____

1ST QUARTER	2ND QUARTER	3RD QUARTER	4TH QUARTER
WEEK 1	WEEK 10	WEEK 19	WEEK 28
WEEK 2	WEEK 11	WEEK 20	WEEK 29
WEEK 3	WEEK 12	WEEK 21	WEEK 30
WEEK 4	WEEK 13	WEEK 22	WEEK 31
WEEK 5	WEEK 14	WEEK 23	WEEK 32
WEEK 6	WEEK 15	WEEK 24	WEEK 33
WEEK 7	WEEK 16	WEEK 25	WEEK 34
WEEK 8	WEEK 17	WEEK 26	WEEK 35
WEEK 9	WEEK 18	WEEK 27	WEEK 36

YEARLY OVERVIEW

STUDENT: _____

1ST QUARTER	2ND QUARTER	3RD QUARTER	4TH QUARTER
WEEK 1	WEEK 10	WEEK 19	WEEK 28
WEEK 2	WEEK 11	WEEK 20	WEEK 29
WEEK 3	WEEK 12	WEEK 21	WEEK 30
WEEK 4	WEEK 13	WEEK 22	WEEK 31
WEEK 5	WEEK 14	WEEK 23	WEEK 32
WEEK 6	WEEK 15	WEEK 24	WEEK 33
WEEK 7	WEEK 16	WEEK 25	WEEK 34
WEEK 8	WEEK 17	WEEK 26	WEEK 35
WEEK 9	WEEK 18	WEEK 27	WEEK 36

STUDENT: _____

YEARLY OVERVIEW

1ST QUARTER	2ND QUARTER	3RD QUARTER	4TH QUARTER
WEEK 1	WEEK 10	WEEK 19	WEEK 28
WEEK 2	WEEK 11	WEEK 20	WEEK 29
WEEK 3	WEEK 12	WEEK 21	WEEK 30
WEEK 4	WEEK 13	WEEK 22	WEEK 31
WEEK 5	WEEK 14	WEEK 23	WEEK 32
WEEK 6	WEEK 15	WEEK 24	WEEK 33
WEEK 7	WEEK 16	WEEK 25	WEEK 34
WEEK 8	WEEK 17	WEEK 26	WEEK 35
WEEK 9	WEEK 18	WEEK 27	WEEK 36

STUDENT: _____

WEEKLY SCHEDULE

TIME					

SUBJECT   CURRICULUM

_____   _____
_____   _____
_____   _____
_____   _____
_____   _____
_____   _____
_____   _____

STUDENT: _____

WEEKLY SCHEDULE

TIME					

SUBJECT

CURRICULUM

_____ _____

_____ _____

_____ _____

_____ _____

_____ _____

_____ _____

STUDENT: _____

WEEKLY SCHEDULE

TIME					

SUBJECT

CURRICULUM

_____   _____

_____   _____

_____   _____

_____   _____

_____   _____

_____   _____

STUDENT: _____

WEEKLY SCHEDULE

TIME					

SUBJECT

CURRICULUM

STUDENT: _____

WEEKLY SCHEDULE

TIME					

SUBJECT   CURRICULUM

_____   _____
_____   _____
_____   _____
_____   _____
_____   _____
_____   _____
_____   _____

STUDENT: _____

WEEKLY SCHEDULE

TIME					

SUBJECT

CURRICULUM

TEACHER'S MASTER SCHEDULE

MONDAY	TUESDAY	WEDNESDAY
7	7	7
8	8	8
9	9	9
10	10	10
11	11	11
12	12	12
1	1	1
2	2	2
3	3	3
4	4	4
5	5	5
6	6	6
7	7	7
8	8	8
9	9	9

TEACHER'S MASTER SCHEDULE

THURSDAY	FRIDAY	SATURDAY
7	7	
8	8	
9	9	
10	10	
11	11	
12	12	
1	1	
2	2	**SUNDAY**
3	3	
4	4	
5	5	
6	6	
7	7	
8	8	
9	9	

12 MONTHS OF LESSON PLANS

YOU ARE BRAVER THAN
YOU BELIEVE, STRONGER
THAN YOU SEEM AND
SMARTER THAN YOU THINK

———

A.A. MILNE

MONTH 1

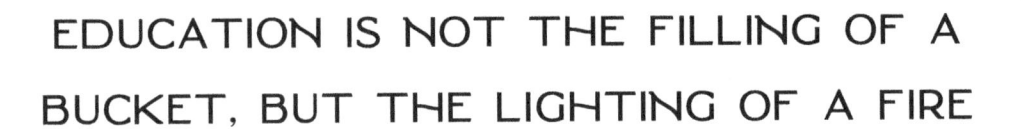

EDUCATION IS NOT THE FILLING OF A BUCKET, BUT THE LIGHTING OF A FIRE

W. B. YEATS

THIS MONTH WE ARE GRATEFUL FOR...

PRAYER REQUESTS & PRAISES

MONTH 1 OVERVIEW

READING LIST	IMPORTANT REMINDERS
•	
•	
•	
•	
•	
•	
•	
•	
•	

SUPPLIES NEEDED	WEBSITES / RESOURCES

MONTH 1 CALENDAR

MONDAY	TUESDAY	WEDNESDAY	THURSDAY

MONTH 1 CALENDAR

FRIDAY	SATURDAY	SUNDAY

HYDRATION: 1 2 3 4 5 6 7 8 9 10 11 12 13 14 15 16 17 18 19 20 21 22 23 24 25 26 27 28 29 30 31

LESSON PLANNER - WEEK 1

	SUBJECT	SUBJECT	SUBJECT	SUBJECT
MON				
TUES				
WED				
THURS				
FRI				

LESSON PLANNER - WEEK 1

SUBJECT	SUBJECT	SUBJECT	NOTES

LESSON PLANNER - WEEK 2

	SUBJECT	SUBJECT	SUBJECT	SUBJECT
MON				
TUES				
WED				
THURS				
FRI				

LESSON PLANNER - WEEK 2

SUBJECT	SUBJECT	SUBJECT	NOTES

LESSON PLANNER - WEEK 3

	SUBJECT	SUBJECT	SUBJECT	SUBJECT
MON				
TUES				
WED				
THURS				
FRI				

LESSON PLANNER - WEEK 3

SUBJECT	SUBJECT	SUBJECT	NOTES

LESSON PLANNER - WEEK 4

	SUBJECT	SUBJECT	SUBJECT	SUBJECT
MON				
TUES				
WED				
THURS				
FRI				

LESSON PLANNER - WEEK 4

SUBJECT	SUBJECT	SUBJECT	NOTES

LESSON PLANNER - WEEK 5

	SUBJECT	SUBJECT	SUBJECT	SUBJECT
MON				
TUES				
WED				
THURS				
FRI				

LESSON PLANNER - WEEK 5

SUBJECT	SUBJECT	SUBJECT	NOTES

MONTH 2

A PERSON WHO NEVER MADE A MISTAKE NEVER TRIED ANYTHING NEW.

ALBERT EINSTEIN

THIS MONTH WE ARE GRATEFUL FOR...

PRAYER REQUESTS & PRAISES

MONTH 2 OVERVIEW

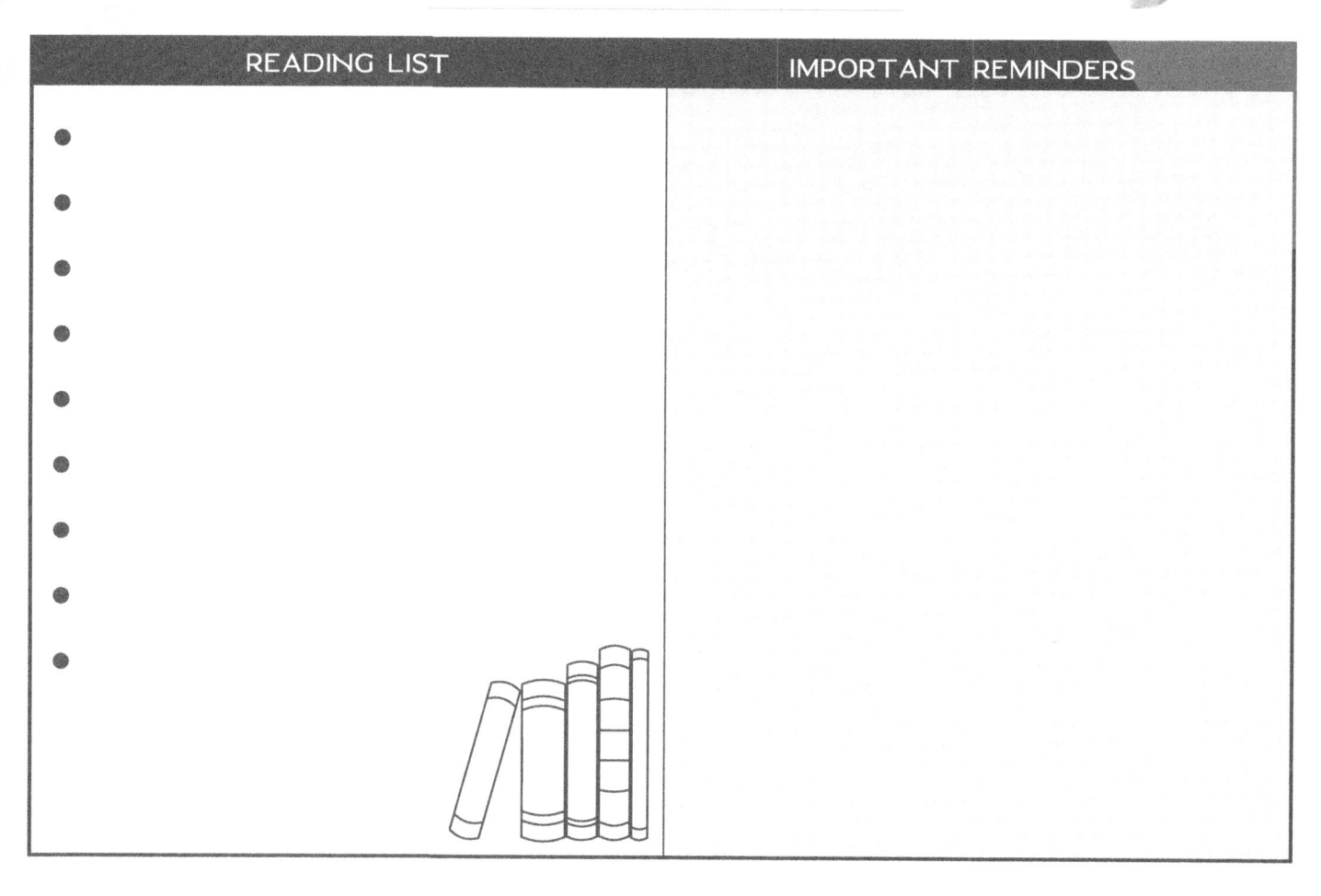

READING LIST	IMPORTANT REMINDERS
•	
•	
•	
•	
•	
•	
•	
•	
•	

SUPPLIES NEEDED

WEBSITES / RESOURCES

MONTH 2 CALENDAR

MONDAY	TUESDAY	WEDNESDAY	THURSDAY

MONTH 2 CALENDAR

FRIDAY	SATURDAY	SUNDAY

HYDRATION: 1 2 3 4 5 6 7 8 9 10 11 12 13 14 15 16 17 18 19 20 21 22 23 24 25 26 27 28 29 30 31

LESSON PLANNER - WEEK 1

	SUBJECT	SUBJECT	SUBJECT	SUBJECT
MON				
TUES				
WED				
THURS				
FRI				

LESSON PLANNER - WEEK 1

SUBJECT	SUBJECT	SUBJECT	NOTES

SUBJECT　　　SUBJECT　　　SUBJECT

LESSON PLANNER - WEEK 2

	SUBJECT	SUBJECT	SUBJECT	SUBJECT
MON				
TUES				
WED				
THURS				
FRI				

LESSON PLANNER - WEEK 2

SUBJECT	SUBJECT	SUBJECT	NOTES

SUBJECT · SUBJECT · SUBJECT

LESSON PLANNER - WEEK 3

	SUBJECT	SUBJECT	SUBJECT	SUBJECT
MON				
TUES				
WED				
THURS				
FRI				

LESSON PLANNER - WEEK 3

SUBJECT	SUBJECT	SUBJECT	NOTES

| SUBJECT | SUBJECT | SUBJECT | |

LESSON PLANNER - WEEK 4

	SUBJECT	SUBJECT	SUBJECT	SUBJECT
MON				
TUES				
WED				
THURS				
FRI				

LESSON PLANNER - WEEK 4

SUBJECT	SUBJECT	SUBJECT	NOTES

LESSON PLANNER - WEEK 5

	SUBJECT	SUBJECT	SUBJECT	SUBJECT
MON				
TUES				
WED				
THURS				
FRI				

LESSON PLANNER - WEEK 5

SUBJECT	SUBJECT	SUBJECT	NOTES

MONTH 3

> NEVER LET THE FEAR OF STRIKING OUT STOP YOU FROM PLAYING THE GAME.
>
> BABE RUTH

THIS MONTH WE ARE GRATEFUL FOR...

PRAYER REQUESTS & PRAISES

MONTH 3 OVERVIEW

READING LIST	IMPORTANT REMINDERS
•	
•	
•	
•	
•	
•	
•	
•	
•	

SUPPLIES NEEDED

WEBSITES / RESOURCES

MONTH 3 CALENDAR

MONDAY	TUESDAY	WEDNESDAY	THURSDAY

MONTH 3 CALENDAR

FRIDAY	SATURDAY	SUNDAY

HYDRATION: 1 2 3 4 5 6 7 8 9 10 11 12 13 14 15 16 17 18 19 20 21 22 23 24 25 26 27 28 29 30 31

LESSON PLANNER - WEEK 1

	SUBJECT	SUBJECT	SUBJECT	SUBJECT
MON				
TUES				
WED				
THURS				
FRI				

LESSON PLANNER - WEEK 1

SUBJECT	SUBJECT	SUBJECT	NOTES

SUBJECT　　SUBJECT　　SUBJECT

LESSON PLANNER - WEEK 2

	SUBJECT	SUBJECT	SUBJECT	SUBJECT
MON				
TUES				
WED				
THURS				
FRI				

LESSON PLANNER - WEEK 2

SUBJECT	SUBJECT	SUBJECT	NOTES

| SUBJECT | SUBJECT | SUBJECT |

LESSON PLANNER - WEEK 3

	SUBJECT	SUBJECT	SUBJECT	SUBJECT
MON				
TUES				
WED				
THURS				
FRI				

LESSON PLANNER - WEEK 3

SUBJECT	SUBJECT	SUBJECT	NOTES

LESSON PLANNER - WEEK 4

	SUBJECT	SUBJECT	SUBJECT	SUBJECT
MON				
TUES				
WED				
THURS				
FRI				

LESSON PLANNER - WEEK 4

SUBJECT	SUBJECT	SUBJECT	NOTES

LESSON PLANNER - WEEK 5

	SUBJECT	SUBJECT	SUBJECT	SUBJECT
MON				
TUES				
WED				
THURS				
FRI				

LESSON PLANNER - WEEK 5

SUBJECT	SUBJECT	SUBJECT	NOTES

MONTH 4

PROCRASTINATION MAKES EASY THINGS HARD AND HARD THINGS HARDER.

MASON COOLEY

THIS MONTH WE ARE GRATEFUL FOR...

PRAYER REQUESTS & PRAISES

MONTH 4 OVERVIEW

READING LIST

-
-
-
-
-
-
-
-
-

IMPORTANT REMINDERS

SUPPLIES NEEDED

WEBSITES / RESOURCES

MONTH 4 CALENDAR

MONDAY	TUESDAY	WEDNESDAY	THURSDAY

MONTH 4 CALENDAR

FRIDAY	SATURDAY	SUNDAY

HYDRATION: 1 2 3 4 5 6 7 8 9 10 11 12 13 14 15 16 17 18 19 20 21 22 23 24 25 26 27 28 29 30 31

LESSON PLANNER - WEEK 1

	SUBJECT	SUBJECT	SUBJECT	SUBJECT
MON				
TUES				
WED				
THURS				
FRI				

LESSON PLANNER - WEEK 1

SUBJECT	SUBJECT	SUBJECT	NOTES

SUBJECT	SUBJECT	SUBJECT	

LESSON PLANNER - WEEK 2

	SUBJECT	SUBJECT	SUBJECT	SUBJECT
MON				
TUES				
WED				
THURS				
FRI				

LESSON PLANNER - WEEK 2

SUBJECT	SUBJECT	SUBJECT	NOTES

LESSON PLANNER - WEEK 3

	SUBJECT	SUBJECT	SUBJECT	SUBJECT
MON				
TUES				
WED				
THURS				
FRI				

LESSON PLANNER - WEEK 3

SUBJECT	SUBJECT	SUBJECT	NOTES

SUBJECT   SUBJECT   SUBJECT

LESSON PLANNER - WEEK 4

	SUBJECT	SUBJECT	SUBJECT	SUBJECT
MON				
TUES				
WED				
THURS				
FRI				

LESSON PLANNER - WEEK 4

SUBJECT	SUBJECT	SUBJECT	NOTES

LESSON PLANNER - WEEK 5

	SUBJECT	SUBJECT	SUBJECT	SUBJECT
MON				
TUES				
WED				
THURS				
FRI				

LESSON PLANNER - WEEK 5

SUBJECT	SUBJECT	SUBJECT	NOTES

MONTH 5

> YOU DON'T HAVE TO BE GREAT TO START,
> BUT YOU HAVE TO START TO BE GREAT.
>
> ZIG ZIGLAR

THIS MONTH WE ARE GRATEFUL FOR...

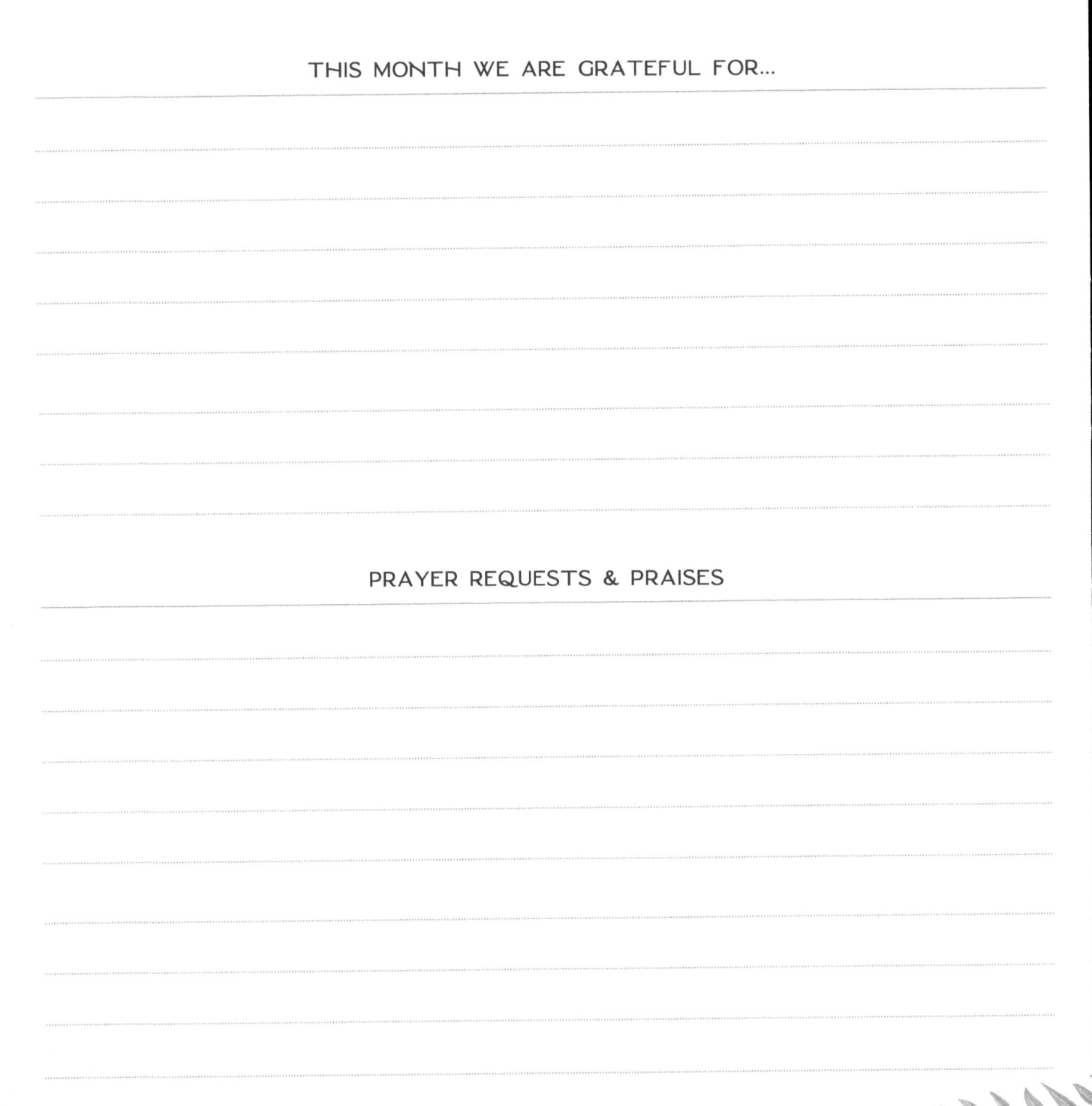

PRAYER REQUESTS & PRAISES

MONTH 5 OVERVIEW

READING LIST

-
-
-
-
-
-
-
-
-

IMPORTANT REMINDERS

SUPPLIES NEEDED

WEBSITES / RESOURCES

MONTH 5 CALENDAR

MONDAY	TUESDAY	WEDNESDAY	THURSDAY

MONTH 5 CALENDAR

FRIDAY	SATURDAY	SUNDAY

HYDRATION: 1 2 3 4 5 6 7 8 9 10 11 12 13 14 15 16 17 18 19 20 21 22 23 24 25 26 27 28 29 30 31

LESSON PLANNER - WEEK 1

	SUBJECT	SUBJECT	SUBJECT	SUBJECT
MON				
TUES				
WED				
THURS				
FRI				

LESSON PLANNER - WEEK 1

SUBJECT	SUBJECT	SUBJECT	NOTES

LESSON PLANNER - WEEK 2

	SUBJECT	SUBJECT	SUBJECT	SUBJECT
MON				
TUES				
WED				
THURS				
FRI				

LESSON PLANNER - WEEK 2

SUBJECT	SUBJECT	SUBJECT	NOTES

LESSON PLANNER - WEEK 3

	SUBJECT	SUBJECT	SUBJECT	SUBJECT
MON				
TUES				
WED				
THURS				
FRI				

LESSON PLANNER - WEEK 3

SUBJECT	SUBJECT	SUBJECT	NOTES

| SUBJECT | SUBJECT | SUBJECT |

LESSON PLANNER - WEEK 4

	SUBJECT	SUBJECT	SUBJECT	SUBJECT
MON				
TUES				
WED				
THURS				
FRI				

LESSON PLANNER - WEEK 4

SUBJECT	SUBJECT	SUBJECT	NOTES

LESSON PLANNER - WEEK 5

	SUBJECT	SUBJECT	SUBJECT	SUBJECT
MON				
TUES				
WED				
THURS				
FRI				

LESSON PLANNER - WEEK 5

SUBJECT	SUBJECT	SUBJECT	NOTES

SUBJECT   SUBJECT   SUBJECT

MONTH 6

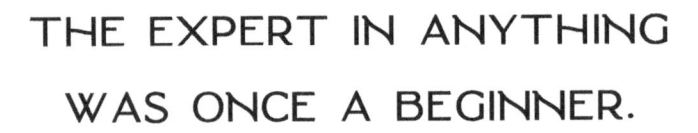

THE EXPERT IN ANYTHING WAS ONCE A BEGINNER.

HELEN HAYES

THIS MONTH WE ARE GRATEFUL FOR...

PRAYER REQUESTS & PRAISES

MONTH 6 OVERVIEW

READING LIST

IMPORTANT REMINDERS

SUPPLIES NEEDED

WEBSITES / RESOURCES

MONTH 6 CALENDAR

MONDAY	TUESDAY	WEDNESDAY	THURSDAY

MONTH 6 CALENDAR

FRIDAY	SATURDAY	SUNDAY

HYDRATION: 1 2 3 4 5 6 7 8 9 10 11 12 13 14 15 16 17 18 19 20 21 22 23 24 25 26 27 28 29 30 31

LESSON PLANNER - WEEK 1

	SUBJECT	SUBJECT	SUBJECT	SUBJECT
MON				
TUES				
WED				
THURS				
FRI				

LESSON PLANNER - WEEK 1

SUBJECT	SUBJECT	SUBJECT	NOTES

LESSON PLANNER - WEEK 2

	SUBJECT	SUBJECT	SUBJECT	SUBJECT
MON				
TUES				
WED				
THURS				
FRI				

LESSON PLANNER - WEEK 2

SUBJECT	SUBJECT	SUBJECT	NOTES

SUBJECT	SUBJECT	SUBJECT

LESSON PLANNER - WEEK 3

	SUBJECT	SUBJECT	SUBJECT	SUBJECT
MON				
TUES				
WED				
THURS				
FRI				

LESSON PLANNER - WEEK 3

SUBJECT	SUBJECT	SUBJECT	NOTES

SUBJECT · SUBJECT · SUBJECT

LESSON PLANNER - WEEK 4

	SUBJECT	SUBJECT	SUBJECT	SUBJECT
MON				
TUES				
WED				
THURS				
FRI				

LESSON PLANNER - WEEK 4

SUBJECT	SUBJECT	SUBJECT	NOTES

LESSON PLANNER - WEEK 5

	SUBJECT	SUBJECT	SUBJECT	SUBJECT
MON				
TUES				
WED				
THURS				
FRI				

LESSON PLANNER - WEEK 5

SUBJECT	SUBJECT	SUBJECT	NOTES

SUBJECT SUBJECT SUBJECT

MONTH 7

THE WAY TO GET STARTED IS TO QUIT TALKING AND BEGIN DOING.

WALT DISNEY

THIS MONTH WE ARE GRATEFUL FOR...

PRAYER REQUESTS & PRAISES

MONTH 7 OVERVIEW

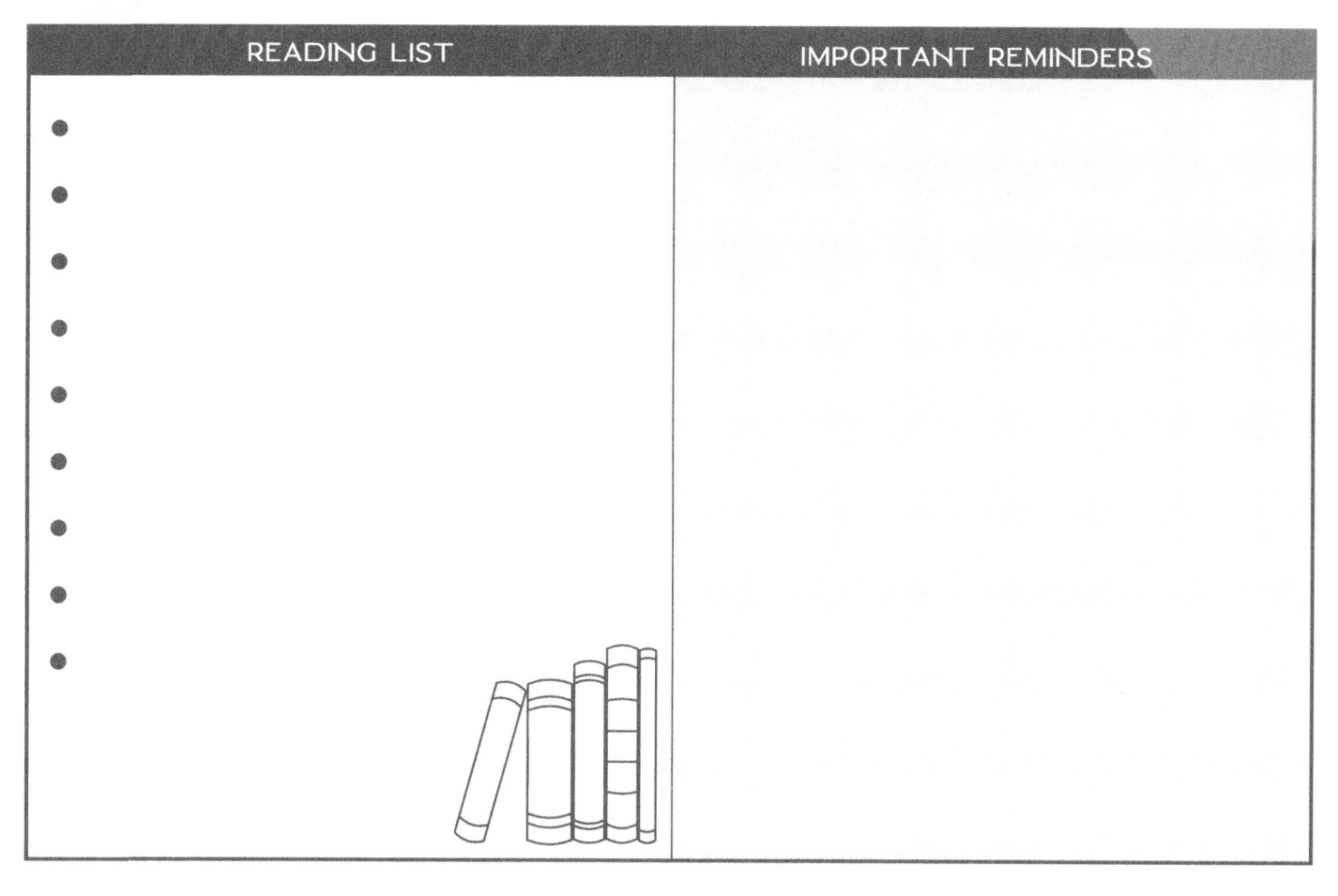

READING LIST

-
-
-
-
-
-
-
-
-

IMPORTANT REMINDERS

SUPPLIES NEEDED

WEBSITES / RESOURCES

MONTH 7 CALENDAR

MONDAY	TUESDAY	WEDNESDAY	THURSDAY

MONTH 7 CALENDAR

FRIDAY	SATURDAY	SUNDAY

HYDRATION: 1 2 3 4 5 6 7 8 9 10 11 12 13 14 15 16 17 18 19 20 21 22 23 24 25 26 27 28 29 30 31

LESSON PLANNER - WEEK 1

	SUBJECT	SUBJECT	SUBJECT	SUBJECT
MON				
TUES				
WED				
THURS				
FRI				

LESSON PLANNER - WEEK 1

SUBJECT	SUBJECT	SUBJECT	NOTES

| SUBJECT | SUBJECT | SUBJECT |

LESSON PLANNER - WEEK 2

	SUBJECT	SUBJECT	SUBJECT	SUBJECT
MON				
TUES				
WED				
THURS				
FRI				

LESSON PLANNER - WEEK 2

| SUBJECT | SUBJECT | SUBJECT | NOTES |

LESSON PLANNER - WEEK 3

	SUBJECT	SUBJECT	SUBJECT	SUBJECT
MON				
TUES				
WED				
THURS				
FRI				

LESSON PLANNER - WEEK 3

SUBJECT	SUBJECT	SUBJECT	NOTES

LESSON PLANNER - WEEK 4

	SUBJECT	SUBJECT	SUBJECT	SUBJECT
MON				
TUES				
WED				
THURS				
FRI				

LESSON PLANNER - WEEK 4

SUBJECT	SUBJECT	SUBJECT	NOTES

LESSON PLANNER - WEEK 5

	SUBJECT	SUBJECT	SUBJECT	SUBJECT
MON				
TUES				
WED				
THURS				
FRI				

LESSON PLANNER - WEEK 5

SUBJECT	SUBJECT	SUBJECT	NOTES

MONTH 8

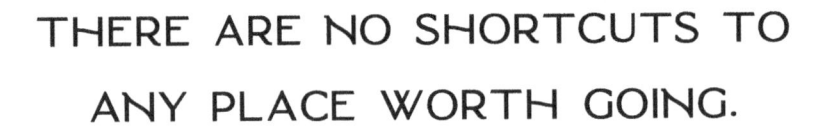

THERE ARE NO SHORTCUTS TO ANY PLACE WORTH GOING.

BEVERLY STILLS

THIS MONTH WE ARE GRATEFUL FOR...

PRAYER REQUESTS & PRAISES

MONTH 8 OVERVIEW

READING LIST

-
-
-
-
-
-
-
-
-

IMPORTANT REMINDERS

SUPPLIES NEEDED

WEBSITES / RESOURCES

MONTH 8 CALENDAR

MONDAY	TUESDAY	WEDNESDAY	THURSDAY

MONTH 8 CALENDAR

FRIDAY	SATURDAY	SUNDAY

HYDRATION 1 2 3 4 5 6 7 8 9 10 11 12 13 14 15 16 17 18 19 20 21 22 23 24 25 26 27 28 29 30 31

LESSON PLANNER - WEEK 1

	SUBJECT	SUBJECT	SUBJECT	SUBJECT
MON				
TUES				
WED				
THURS				
FRI				

LESSON PLANNER - WEEK 1

SUBJECT   SUBJECT   SUBJECT   NOTES

LESSON PLANNER - WEEK 2

	SUBJECT	SUBJECT	SUBJECT	SUBJECT
MON				
TUES				
WED				
THURS				
FRI				

LESSON PLANNER - WEEK 2

SUBJECT	SUBJECT	SUBJECT	NOTES

LESSON PLANNER - WEEK 3

	SUBJECT	SUBJECT	SUBJECT	SUBJECT
MON				
TUES				
WED				
THURS				
FRI				

LESSON PLANNER - WEEK 3

| SUBJECT | SUBJECT | SUBJECT | NOTES |

LESSON PLANNER - WEEK 4

	SUBJECT	SUBJECT	SUBJECT	SUBJECT
MON				
TUES				
WED				
THURS				
FRI				

LESSON PLANNER - WEEK 4

SUBJECT	SUBJECT	SUBJECT	NOTES

LESSON PLANNER - WEEK 5

	SUBJECT	SUBJECT	SUBJECT	SUBJECT
MON				
TUES				
WED				
THURS				
FRI				

LESSON PLANNER - WEEK 5

SUBJECT	SUBJECT	SUBJECT	NOTES

MONTH 9

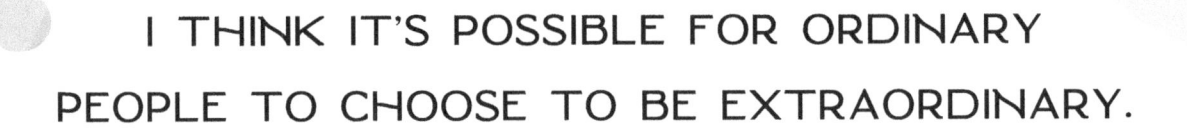

> **I THINK IT'S POSSIBLE FOR ORDINARY PEOPLE TO CHOOSE TO BE EXTRAORDINARY.**
>
> ELON MUSK

THIS MONTH WE ARE GRATEFUL FOR...

PRAYER REQUESTS & PRAISES

MONTH 9 OVERVIEW

READING LIST

-
-
-
-
-
-
-
-
-

IMPORTANT REMINDERS

SUPPLIES NEEDED

WEBSITES / RESOURCES

MONTH 9 CALENDAR

MONDAY	TUESDAY	WEDNESDAY	THURSDAY

MONTH 9 CALENDAR

FRIDAY	SATURDAY	SUNDAY

HYDRATION: 1 2 3 4 5 6 7 8 9 10 11 12 13 14 15 16 17 18 19 20 21 22 23 24 25 26 27 28 29 30 31

LESSON PLANNER - WEEK 1

	SUBJECT	SUBJECT	SUBJECT	SUBJECT
MON				
TUES				
WED				
THURS				
FRI				

LESSON PLANNER - WEEK 1

SUBJECT	SUBJECT	SUBJECT	NOTES

LESSON PLANNER - WEEK 2

	SUBJECT	SUBJECT	SUBJECT	SUBJECT
MON				
TUES				
WED				
THURS				
FRI				

LESSON PLANNER - WEEK 2

SUBJECT	SUBJECT	SUBJECT	NOTES

LESSON PLANNER - WEEK 3

	SUBJECT	SUBJECT	SUBJECT	SUBJECT
MON				
TUES				
WED				
THURS				
FRI				

LESSON PLANNER - WEEK 3

SUBJECT	SUBJECT	SUBJECT	NOTES

LESSON PLANNER - WEEK 4

	SUBJECT	SUBJECT	SUBJECT	SUBJECT
MON				
TUES				
WED				
THURS				
FRI				

LESSON PLANNER - WEEK 4

SUBJECT	SUBJECT	SUBJECT	NOTES

LESSON PLANNER - WEEK 5

	SUBJECT	SUBJECT	SUBJECT	SUBJECT
MON				
TUES				
WED				
THURS				
FRI				

LESSON PLANNER - WEEK 5

SUBJECT	SUBJECT	SUBJECT	NOTES

MONTH 10

> I FIND THAT THE HARDER I WORK,
> THE MORE LUCK I SEEM TO HAVE.
>
> THOMAS JEFFERSON

THIS MONTH WE ARE GRATEFUL FOR...

PRAYER REQUESTS & PRAISES

MONTH 10 OVERVIEW

READING LIST

IMPORTANT REMINDERS

SUPPLIES NEEDED

WEBSITES / RESOURCES

MONTH 10 CALENDAR

MONDAY	TUESDAY	WEDNESDAY	THURSDAY

MONTH 10 CALENDAR

FRIDAY	SATURDAY	SUNDAY

HYDRATION: 1 2 3 4 5 6 7 8 9 10 11 12 13 14 15 16 17 18 19 20 21 22 23 24 25 26 27 28 29 30 31

LESSON PLANNER - WEEK 1

	SUBJECT	SUBJECT	SUBJECT	SUBJECT
MON				
TUES				
WED				
THURS				
FRI				

LESSON PLANNER - WEEK 1

SUBJECT	SUBJECT	SUBJECT	NOTES

LESSON PLANNER - WEEK 2

	SUBJECT	SUBJECT	SUBJECT	SUBJECT
MON				
TUES				
WED				
THURS				
FRI				

LESSON PLANNER - WEEK 2

SUBJECT	SUBJECT	SUBJECT	NOTES

LESSON PLANNER - WEEK 3

	SUBJECT	SUBJECT	SUBJECT	SUBJECT
MON				
TUES				
WED				
THURS				
FRI				

LESSON PLANNER - WEEK 3

SUBJECT	SUBJECT	SUBJECT	NOTES

LESSON PLANNER - WEEK 4

	SUBJECT	SUBJECT	SUBJECT	SUBJECT
MON				
TUES				
WED				
THURS				
FRI				

LESSON PLANNER - WEEK 4

SUBJECT	SUBJECT	SUBJECT	NOTES

SUBJECT   SUBJECT   SUBJECT

LESSON PLANNER - WEEK 5

	SUBJECT	SUBJECT	SUBJECT	SUBJECT
MON				
TUES				
WED				
THURS				
FRI				

LESSON PLANNER - WEEK 5

SUBJECT	SUBJECT	SUBJECT	NOTES

MONTH 11

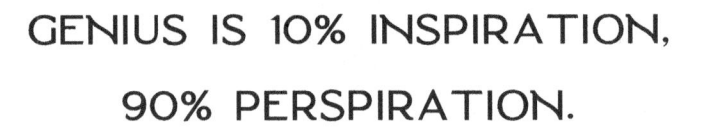

GENIUS IS 10% INSPIRATION, 90% PERSPIRATION.

THOMAS EDISON

THIS MONTH WE ARE GRATEFUL FOR...

PRAYER REQUESTS & PRAISES

MONTH 11 OVERVIEW

READING LIST

-
-
-
-
-
-
-
-
-

IMPORTANT REMINDERS

SUPPLIES NEEDED

WEBSITES / RESOURCES

MONTH 11 CALENDAR

MONDAY	TUESDAY	WEDNESDAY	THURSDAY

MONTH 11 CALENDAR

FRIDAY	SATURDAY	SUNDAY

HYDRATION: 1 2 3 4 5 6 7 8 9 10 11 12 13 14 15 16 17 18 19 20 21 22 23 24 25 26 27 28 29 30 31

LESSON PLANNER - WEEK 1

	SUBJECT	SUBJECT	SUBJECT	SUBJECT
MON				
TUES				
WED				
THURS				
FRI				

LESSON PLANNER - WEEK 1

SUBJECT	SUBJECT	SUBJECT	NOTES

LESSON PLANNER - WEEK 2

	SUBJECT	SUBJECT	SUBJECT	SUBJECT
MON				
TUES				
WED				
THURS				
FRI				

LESSON PLANNER - WEEK 2

SUBJECT	SUBJECT	SUBJECT	NOTES

LESSON PLANNER - WEEK 3

	SUBJECT	SUBJECT	SUBJECT	SUBJECT
MON				
TUES				
WED				
THURS				
FRI				

LESSON PLANNER - WEEK 3

SUBJECT	SUBJECT	SUBJECT	NOTES

LESSON PLANNER - WEEK 4

	SUBJECT	SUBJECT	SUBJECT	SUBJECT
MON				
TUES				
WED				
THURS				
FRI				

LESSON PLANNER - WEEK 4

SUBJECT	SUBJECT	SUBJECT	NOTES

LESSON PLANNER - WEEK 5

	SUBJECT	SUBJECT	SUBJECT	SUBJECT
MON				
TUES				
WED				
THURS				
FRI				

LESSON PLANNER - WEEK 5

SUBJECT	SUBJECT	SUBJECT	NOTES

MONTH 12

> MOTIVATION IS WHAT GETS YOU STARTED.
> HABIT IS WHAT KEEPS YOU GOING.
>
> JIM RYUN

THIS MONTH WE ARE GRATEFUL FOR...

PRAYER REQUESTS & PRAISES

MONTH 12 OVERVIEW

READING LIST

-
-
-
-
-
-
-
-
-

IMPORTANT REMINDERS

SUPPLIES NEEDED

WEBSITES / RESOURCES

MONTH 12 CALENDAR

MONDAY	TUESDAY	WEDNESDAY	THURSDAY

MONTH 12 CALENDAR

FRIDAY	SATURDAY	SUNDAY

HYDRATION: 1 2 3 4 5 6 7 8 9 10 11 12 13 14 15 16 17 18 19 20 21 22 23 24 25 26 27 28 29 30 31

LESSON PLANNER - WEEK 1

	SUBJECT	SUBJECT	SUBJECT	SUBJECT
MON				
TUES				
WED				
THURS				
FRI				

LESSON PLANNER - WEEK 1

SUBJECT	SUBJECT	SUBJECT	NOTES

LESSON PLANNER - WEEK 2

	SUBJECT	SUBJECT	SUBJECT	SUBJECT
MON				
TUES				
WED				
THURS				
FRI				

LESSON PLANNER - WEEK 2

SUBJECT	SUBJECT	SUBJECT	NOTES

LESSON PLANNER - WEEK 3

	SUBJECT	SUBJECT	SUBJECT	SUBJECT
MON				
TUES				
WED				
THURS				
FRI				

LESSON PLANNER - WEEK 3

SUBJECT	SUBJECT	SUBJECT	NOTES

LESSON PLANNER - WEEK 4

	SUBJECT	SUBJECT	SUBJECT	SUBJECT
MON				
TUES				
WED				
THURS				
FRI				

LESSON PLANNER - WEEK 4

SUBJECT	SUBJECT	SUBJECT	NOTES

LESSON PLANNER - WEEK 5

	SUBJECT	SUBJECT	SUBJECT	SUBJECT
MON				
TUES				
WED				
THURS				
FRI				

LESSON PLANNER - WEEK 5

SUBJECT	SUBJECT	SUBJECT	NOTES

SUBJECT　　　　SUBJECT　　　　SUBJECT

REFERENCES & RECORDS

LOCAL CITY/COUNTY SCHOOL CONTACT

NAME:
PHONE:
EMAIL:
ADDRESS:

LOCAL/STATE REQUIREMENTS

DAYS OF INSTRUCTION:
CURRICULUMS:

HEALTH & SAFETY:
AFFIDAVITS:
OTHER:

STATUTE/CODE PERMITTING HOMESCHOOL EDUCATION:

EDUCATIONAL WEBSITES

SITE NAME	LINK	USERNAME	PASSWORD

GRADE TRACKER

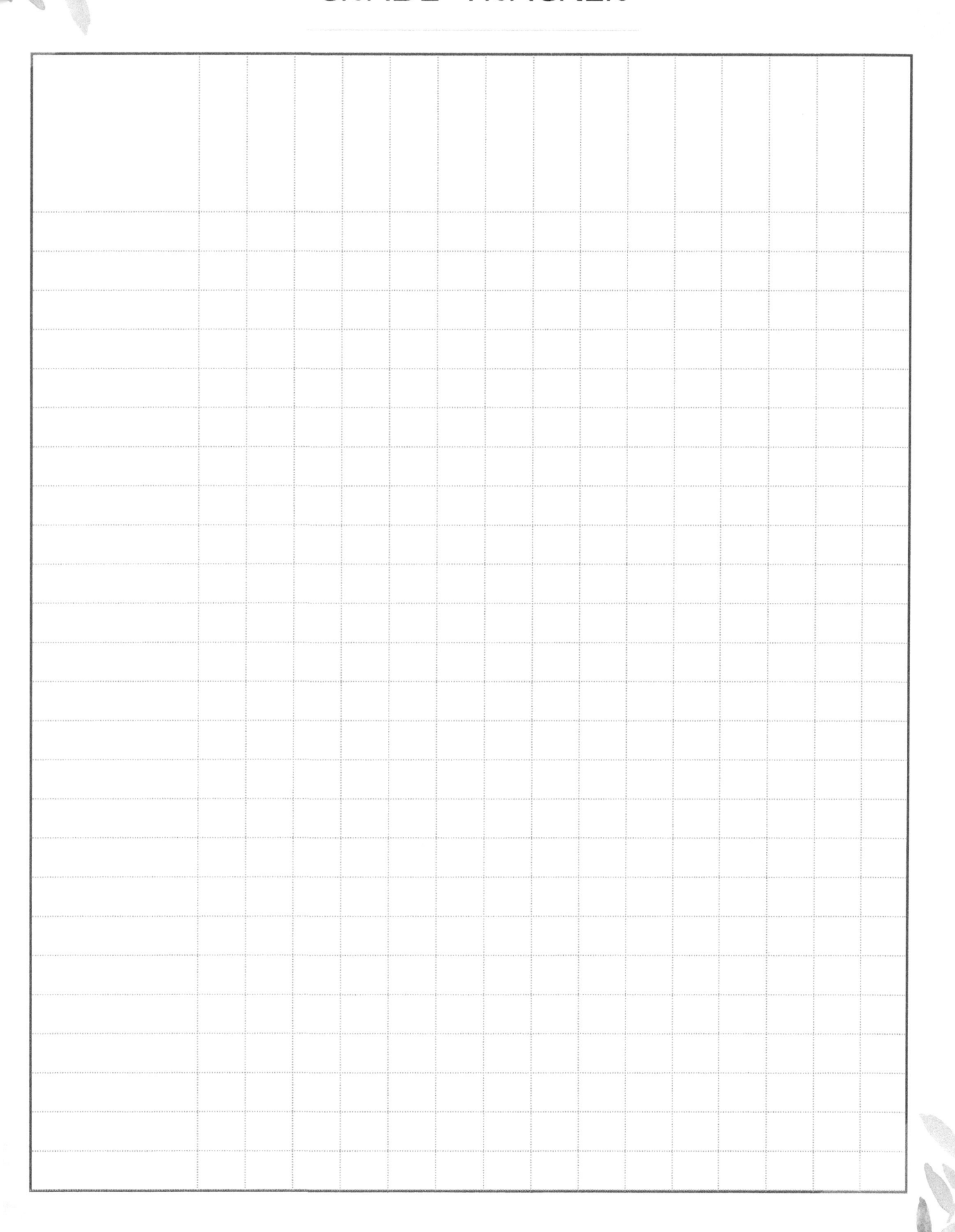

GRADE TRACKER

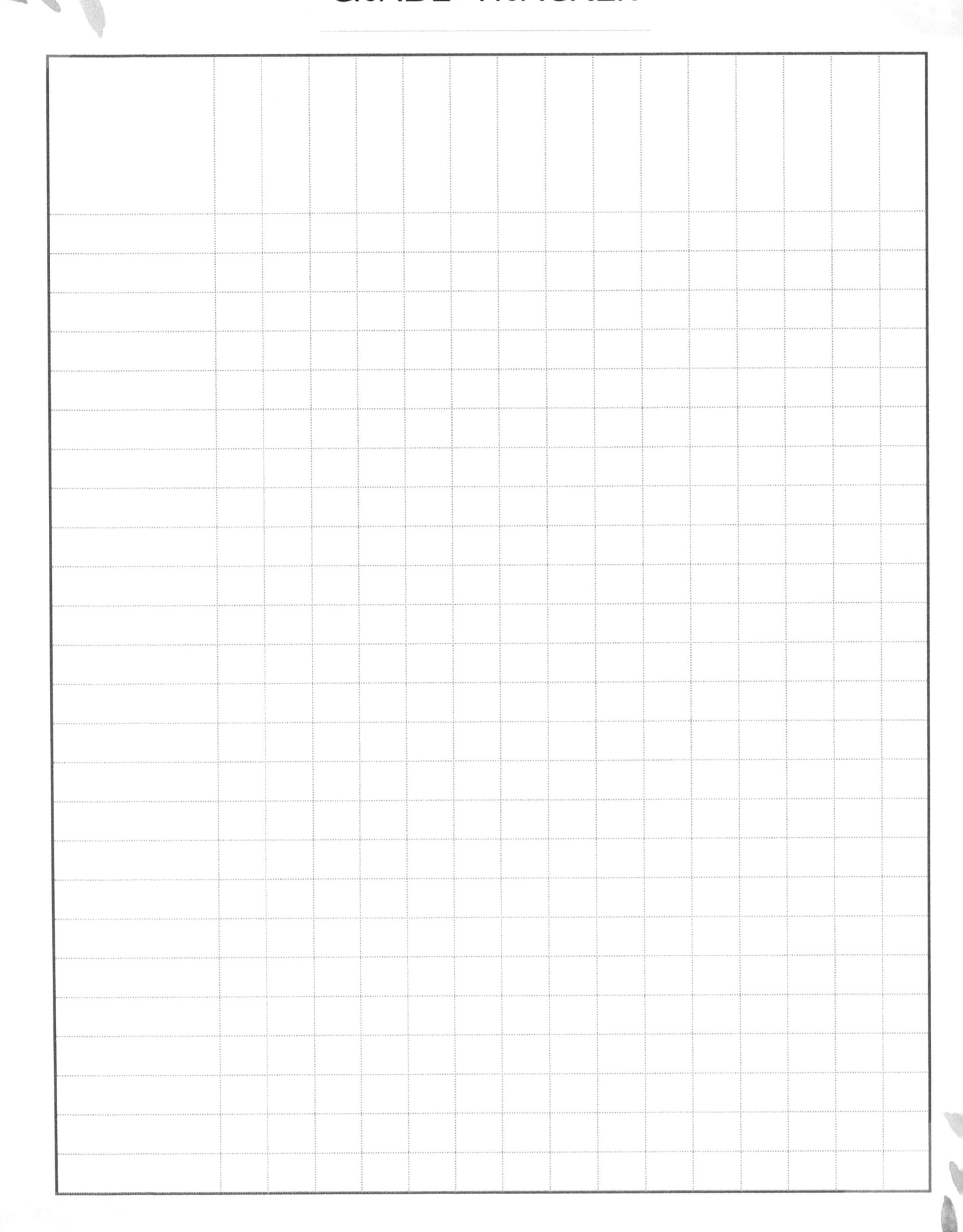

GRADE TRACKER

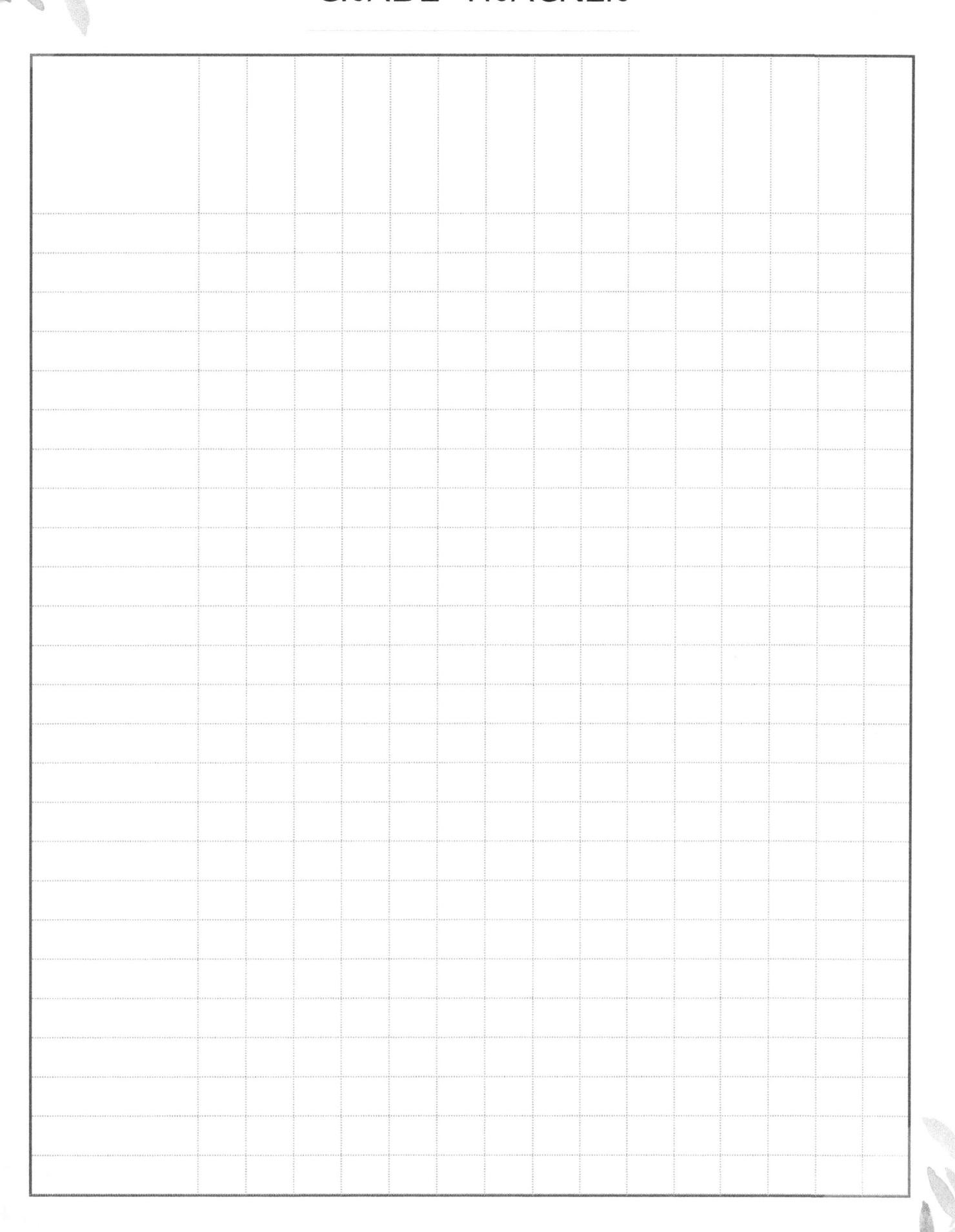

GRADE TRACKER

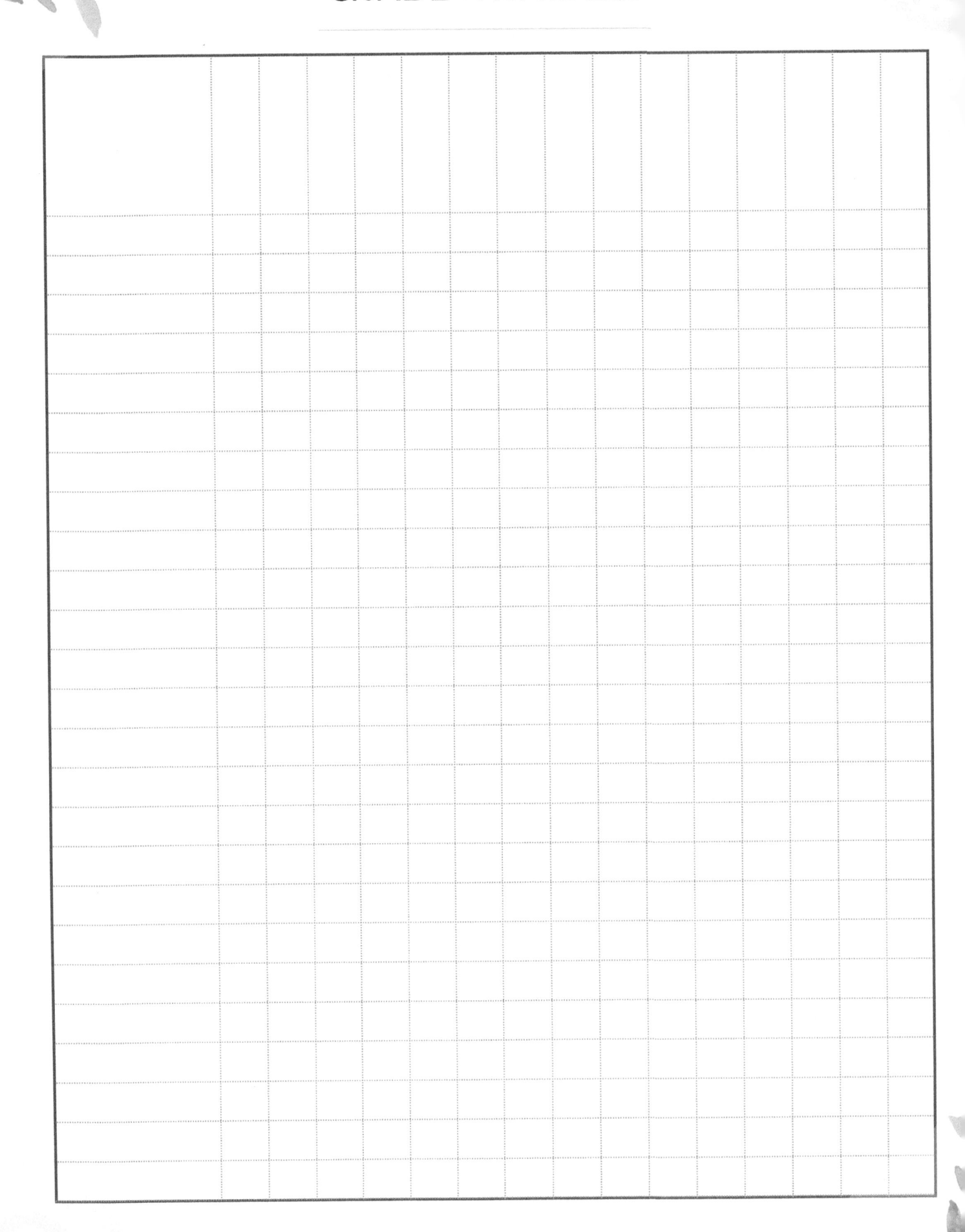

GRADE TRACKER

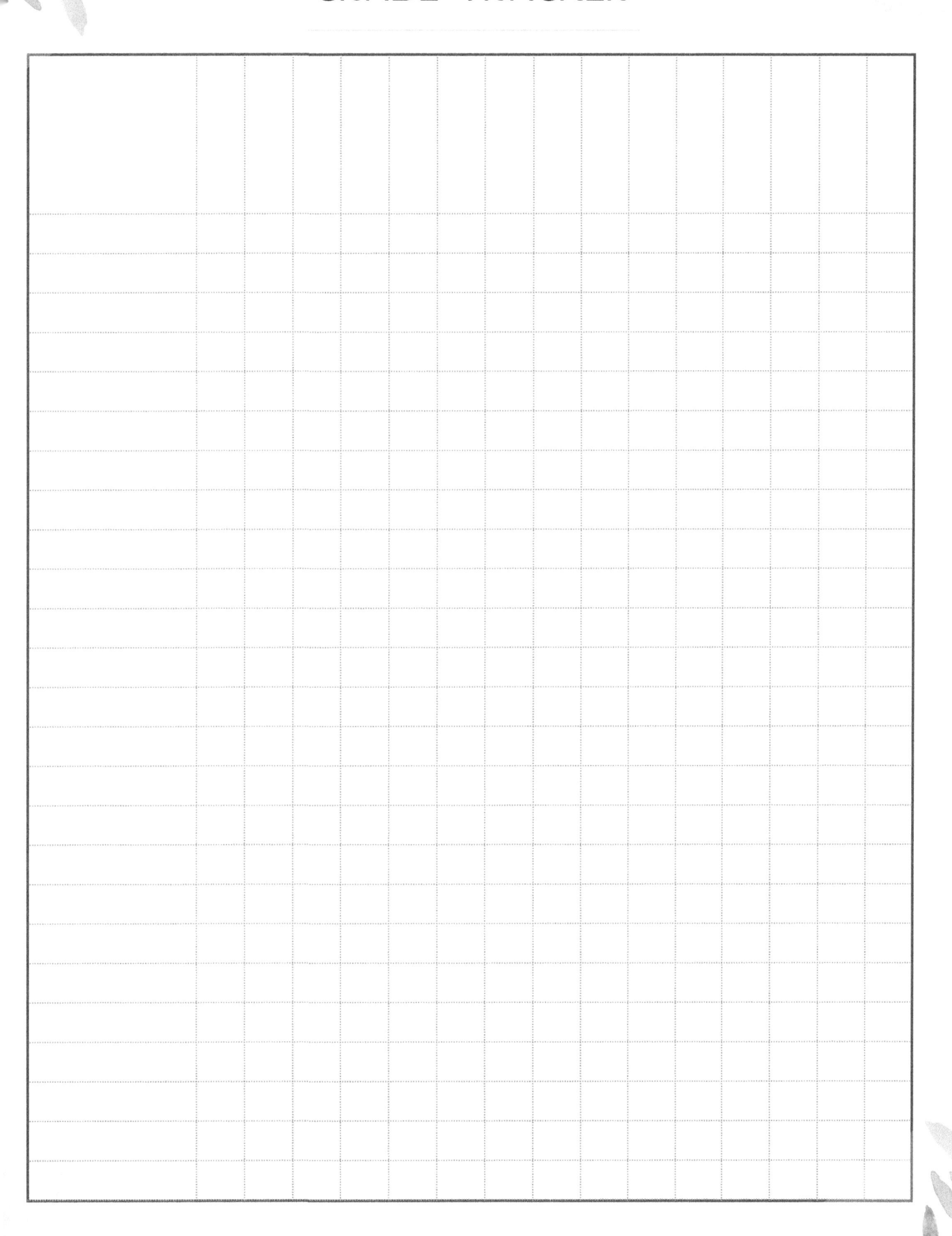

GRADE TRACKER

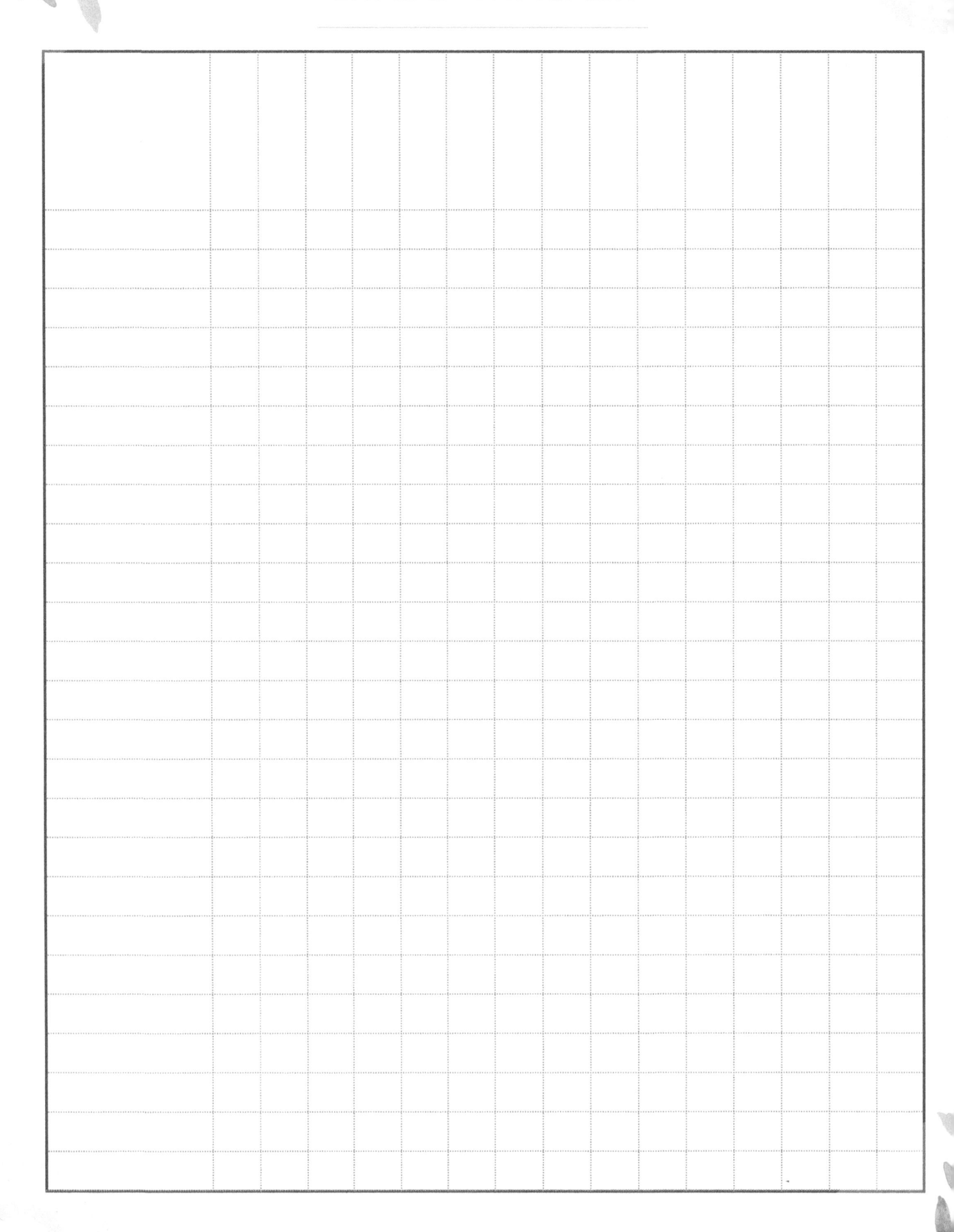

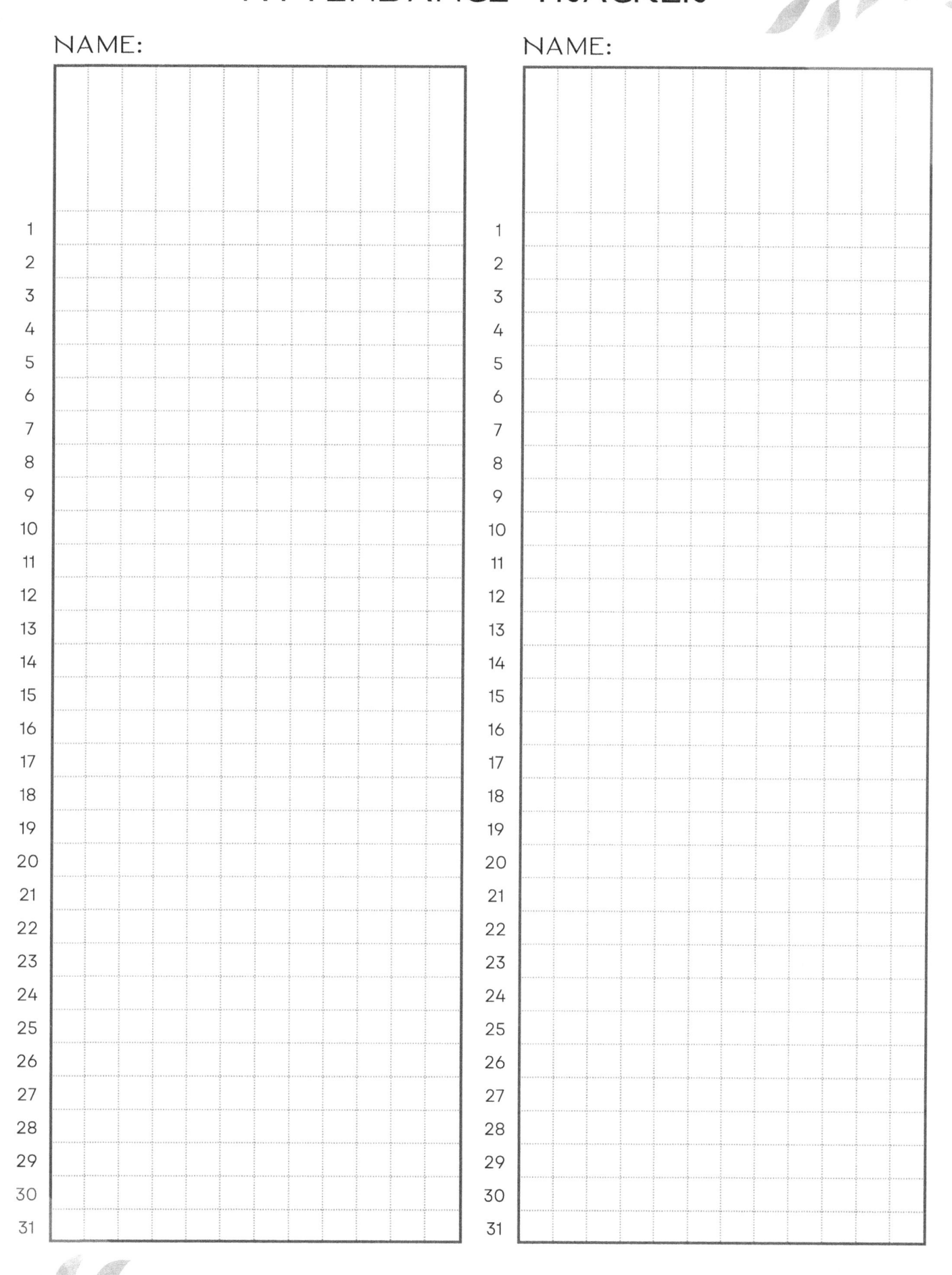

ATTENDANCE TRACKER

NAME:

NAME:

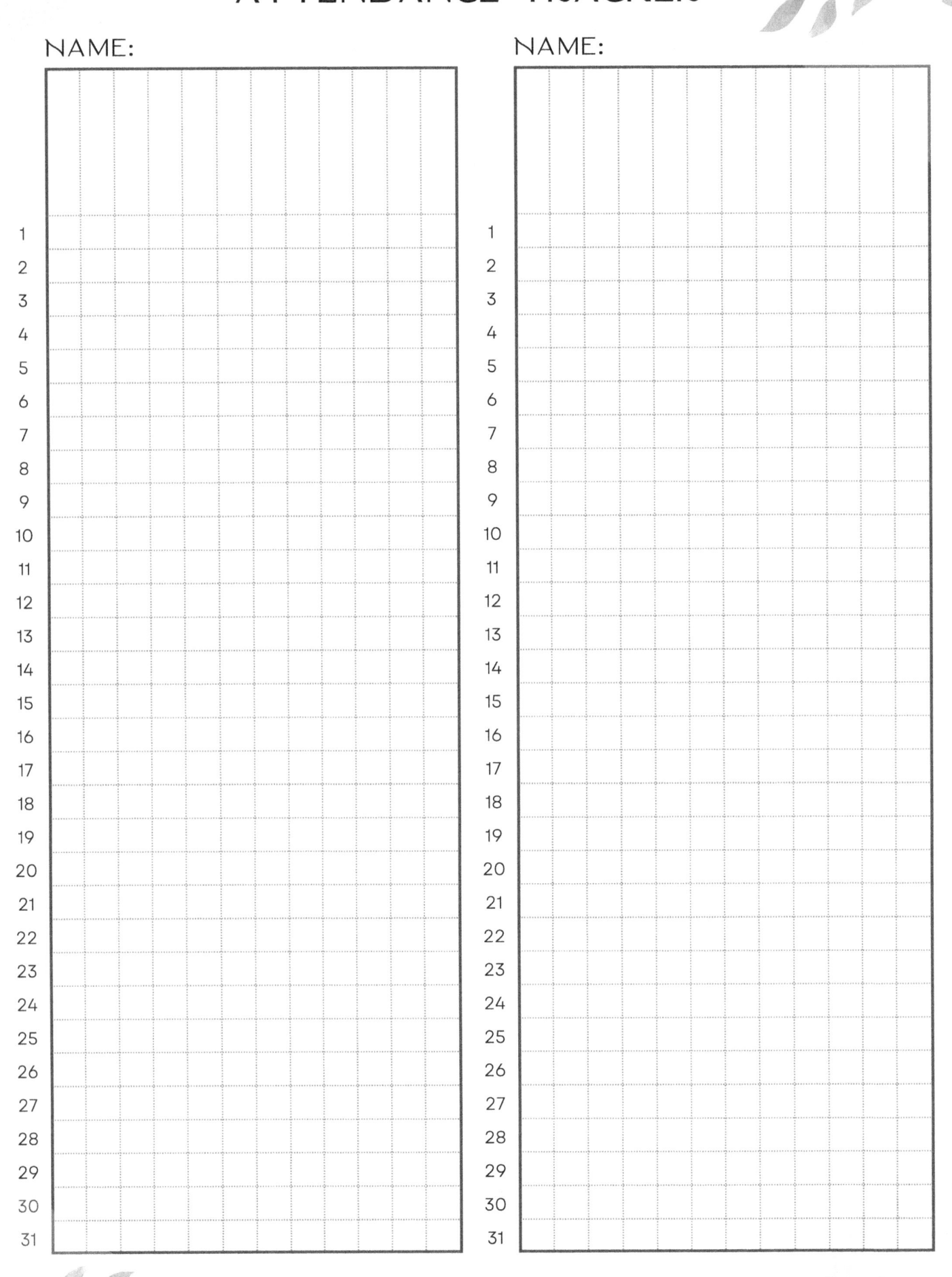

ATTENDANCE TRACKER

NAME:

NAME:

1
2
3
4
5
6
7
8
9
10
11
12
13
14
15
16
17
18
19
20
21
22
23
24
25
26
27
28
29
30
31

ATTENDANCE TRACKER

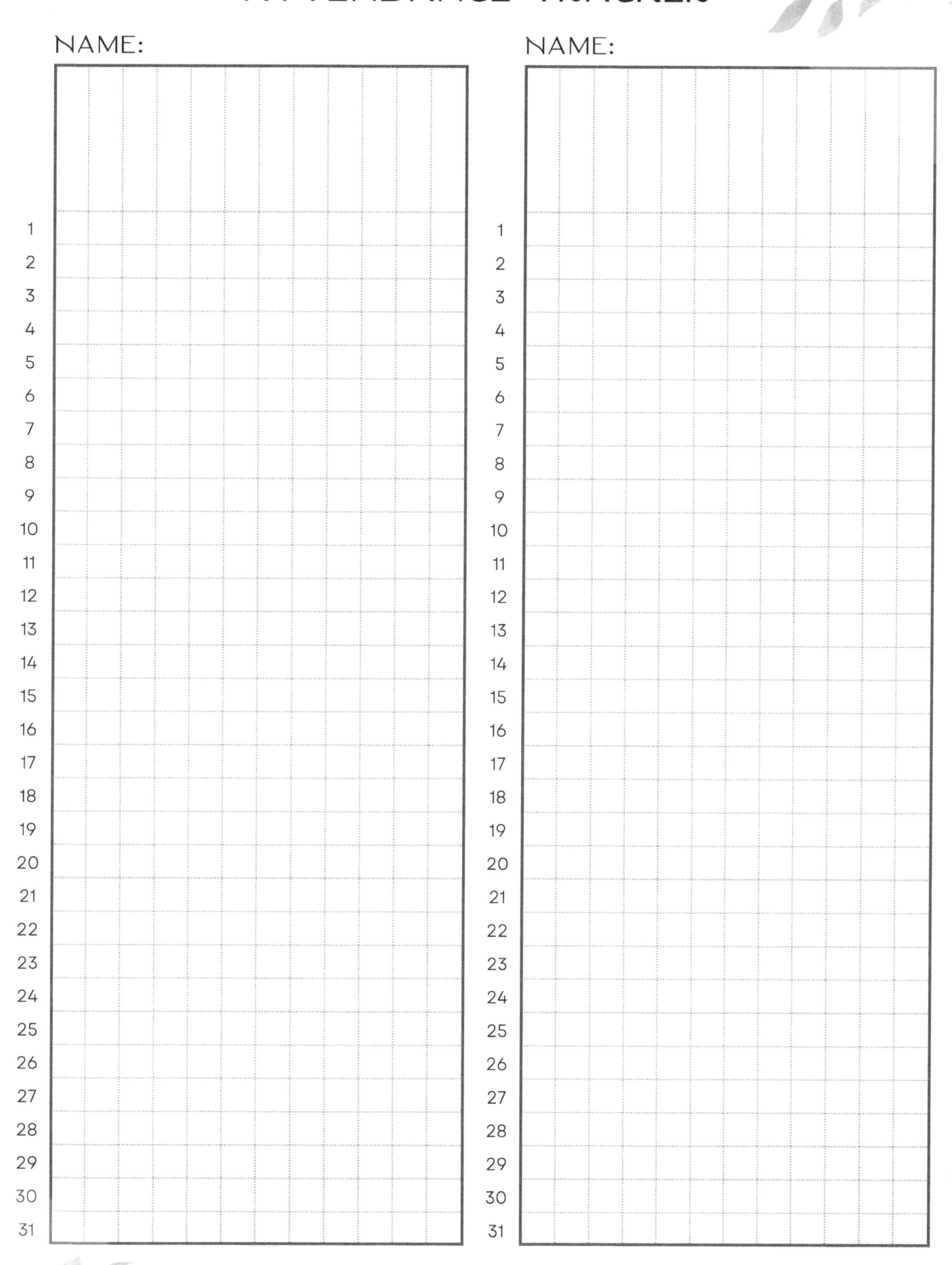

NAME:

NAME:

1
2
3
4
5
6
7
8
9
10
11
12
13
14
15
16
17
18
19
20
21
22
23
24
25
26
27
28
29
30
31

SUCCESS IS THE SUM OF SMALL EFFORTS, REPEATED

R. COLLIER

BOOK LOG

NAME:

BOOK TITLE	AUTHOR	GENRE	RATING
			☆☆☆☆☆
			☆☆☆☆☆
			☆☆☆☆☆
			☆☆☆☆☆
			☆☆☆☆☆
			☆☆☆☆☆
			☆☆☆☆☆
			☆☆☆☆☆
			☆☆☆☆☆
			☆☆☆☆☆
			☆☆☆☆☆
			☆☆☆☆☆
			☆☆☆☆☆
			☆☆☆☆☆
			☆☆☆☆☆
			☆☆☆☆☆
			☆☆☆☆☆
			☆☆☆☆☆
			☆☆☆☆☆
			☆☆☆☆☆
			☆☆☆☆☆
			☆☆☆☆☆
			☆☆☆☆☆
			☆☆☆☆☆
			☆☆☆☆☆
			☆☆☆☆☆
			☆☆☆☆☆
			☆☆☆☆☆

BOOK LOG

NAME:

BOOK TITLE	AUTHOR	GENRE	RATING
			☆☆☆☆☆
			☆☆☆☆☆
			☆☆☆☆☆
			☆☆☆☆☆
			☆☆☆☆☆
			☆☆☆☆☆
			☆☆☆☆☆
			☆☆☆☆☆
			☆☆☆☆☆
			☆☆☆☆☆
			☆☆☆☆☆
			☆☆☆☆☆
			☆☆☆☆☆
			☆☆☆☆☆
			☆☆☆☆☆
			☆☆☆☆☆
			☆☆☆☆☆
			☆☆☆☆☆
			☆☆☆☆☆
			☆☆☆☆☆
			☆☆☆☆☆
			☆☆☆☆☆
			☆☆☆☆☆
			☆☆☆☆☆
			☆☆☆☆☆
			☆☆☆☆☆
			☆☆☆☆☆
			☆☆☆☆☆

BOOK LOG

NAME:

BOOK TITLE	AUTHOR	GENRE	RATING
			☆☆☆☆☆
			☆☆☆☆☆
			☆☆☆☆☆
			☆☆☆☆☆
			☆☆☆☆☆
			☆☆☆☆☆
			☆☆☆☆☆
			☆☆☆☆☆
			☆☆☆☆☆
			☆☆☆☆☆
			☆☆☆☆☆
			☆☆☆☆☆
			☆☆☆☆☆
			☆☆☆☆☆
			☆☆☆☆☆
			☆☆☆☆☆
			☆☆☆☆☆
			☆☆☆☆☆
			☆☆☆☆☆
			☆☆☆☆☆
			☆☆☆☆☆
			☆☆☆☆☆
			☆☆☆☆☆
			☆☆☆☆☆
			☆☆☆☆☆
			☆☆☆☆☆
			☆☆☆☆☆
			☆☆☆☆☆
			☆☆☆☆☆

BOOK LOG

NAME:

BOOK TITLE	AUTHOR	GENRE	RATING
			☆☆☆☆☆
			☆☆☆☆☆
			☆☆☆☆☆
			☆☆☆☆☆
			☆☆☆☆☆
			☆☆☆☆☆
			☆☆☆☆☆
			☆☆☆☆☆
			☆☆☆☆☆
			☆☆☆☆☆
			☆☆☆☆☆
			☆☆☆☆☆
			☆☆☆☆☆
			☆☆☆☆☆
			☆☆☆☆☆
			☆☆☆☆☆
			☆☆☆☆☆
			☆☆☆☆☆
			☆☆☆☆☆
			☆☆☆☆☆
			☆☆☆☆☆
			☆☆☆☆☆
			☆☆☆☆☆
			☆☆☆☆☆
			☆☆☆☆☆
			☆☆☆☆☆
			☆☆☆☆☆
			☆☆☆☆☆
			☆☆☆☆☆
			☆☆☆☆☆

BOOK LOG

NAME:

BOOK TITLE	AUTHOR	GENRE	RATING
			☆☆☆☆☆
			☆☆☆☆☆
			☆☆☆☆☆
			☆☆☆☆☆
			☆☆☆☆☆
			☆☆☆☆☆
			☆☆☆☆☆
			☆☆☆☆☆
			☆☆☆☆☆
			☆☆☆☆☆
			☆☆☆☆☆
			☆☆☆☆☆
			☆☆☆☆☆
			☆☆☆☆☆
			☆☆☆☆☆
			☆☆☆☆☆
			☆☆☆☆☆
			☆☆☆☆☆
			☆☆☆☆☆
			☆☆☆☆☆
			☆☆☆☆☆
			☆☆☆☆☆
			☆☆☆☆☆
			☆☆☆☆☆
			☆☆☆☆☆
			☆☆☆☆☆
			☆☆☆☆☆
			☆☆☆☆☆
			☆☆☆☆☆

BOOK LOG

NAME:

BOOK TITLE	AUTHOR	GENRE	RATING
			☆☆☆☆☆
			☆☆☆☆☆
			☆☆☆☆☆
			☆☆☆☆☆
			☆☆☆☆☆
			☆☆☆☆☆
			☆☆☆☆☆
			☆☆☆☆☆
			☆☆☆☆☆
			☆☆☆☆☆
			☆☆☆☆☆
			☆☆☆☆☆
			☆☆☆☆☆
			☆☆☆☆☆
			☆☆☆☆☆
			☆☆☆☆☆
			☆☆☆☆☆
			☆☆☆☆☆
			☆☆☆☆☆
			☆☆☆☆☆
			☆☆☆☆☆
			☆☆☆☆☆
			☆☆☆☆☆
			☆☆☆☆☆
			☆☆☆☆☆
			☆☆☆☆☆
			☆☆☆☆☆
			☆☆☆☆☆

FAMILY CHORE TRACKER

CHORE	NAME	S	M	T	W	T	F	S

CURRICULUM & SUPPLIES TRACKER

CURRICULUM OR SUPPLIES	COST	SUBJECT OR SUBJECTS	STUDENT(S)

TELL ME AND I FORGET.
TEACH ME AND I REMEMBER.
INVOLVE ME AND I LEARN.

BEN FRANKLIN

OUR HOMESCHOOL FAVORITE
BIBLE VERSES OR QUOTES

Made in the USA
Middletown, DE
21 August 2023